PORTRAIT IN MUSTARD

To Mary Jean Chan

PORTRAIT IN MUSTARD

Wendy Allen

Seren is the book imprint of
Poetry Wales Press Ltd.
Suite 6, 4 Derwen Road, Bridgend, Wales, CF31 1LH
www.serenbooks.com
facebook.com/SerenBooks
twitter@SerenBooks

www.serenbooks.com
facebook.com/SerenBooks
twitter@SerenBooks

The right of Wendy Allen to be identified as
the author of this work has been asserted in accordance
with the Copyright, Designs and Patents Act, 1988.

© Wendy Allen, 2024.

ISBN: 978-1-78172-767-6

A CIP record for this title is available from the British Library.

All rights reserved. No part of this publication may be reproduced,
stored in a retrieval system, or transmitted at any time or by any means,
electronic, mechanical, photocopying, recording or otherwise without
the prior permission of the copyright holder.

The publisher acknowledges the financial assistance of the Books Council of Wales.

Author photograph: Nicholas Hayles.

Cover artwork: Seren Books.

Printed in Bembo by 4Edge Ltd, Hockley.

Contents

7	Cocktail Hour
8	Peach Dress
10	Apricot
11	Tulip
12	coping strategies
13	Sex Life
14	Peach
15	Page 77
16	The Male Curator
17	Appointment
18	Exhibit
19	Portrait in Mustard
22	Service Station
23	Cob Records
24	You Can't Swim in a Gallery
25	If We Were in Llandudno
26	Pleasure Yourself whilst I Watch
27	Des'ree
28	Copenhagen
29	[Self] Floating Form
30	*Acknowledgments and Thanks*

Cocktail Hour

I am about to bend over the bath
I am about to die thinking of your face
underneath me
I am firework inside though you cannot
hear over the sound of the bath water
running   cold   it is mid-November
    you make me come slowly as if you
    know I have waited twenty-four
    years
I am six thirty early evening drunk
I might have ordered a two for one petite
mort cocktail on this date with you
had it actually happened
I would have drunk one straight after I
finished the first
the sweet cherry globe chokes me
    I know my hair looks good

Peach Dress

I am wearing peach, one shoulder showing. Waiting for you to arrive for blank minutes. I am braless, nipples searching for air as they emerge from silk water. My dress is the colour of my pulse beneath *Chanel Chance*.

The tube from Bank to Embankment, then the walk to Southbank to the pretty little kiosk that makes perfect flat whites, takes blank minutes.

The walk to the bar I like that serves vegan peach prosecco, to the Container Hotel where you fucked me in the shower, takes blank minutes.

The forgetting to wait for blank minutes in the foyer of The Hayward Gallery, the standing in Foyles looking at essays, passing time looking at Annie Ernaux's *Simple Passion* whilst outside they clear away the books under the bridge. I always take photos here to send to you and edge them like a polaroid and pretend the photo looked *authentically* like this.

For the past blank years, I've wanted you to buy me the Susan Sontag book on photography so much I have ached. I haven't told you, but I wanted you to know.

The walk over Waterloo Bridge alone like a single scene from a Richard Curtis film, only this film is indie and has Swedish subtitles, is sad and lasts too long.

This dress is made of peaches and the sustainable material lasts as long as the message to you remains undelivered. I wait for you to reply for the next blank hours.

The way the shadows fall over Waterloo Bridge tells me it has been too long for you to be on your way.

Apricot

We discuss the interior of a second, like it is narrative strategy. For you, the second represents only a unit of time. With each millisecond I fall in love with you more. I don't think you know. As your seconds tick, mine are scored open. Inside this apricot, the stone is missing, and I am curled up in the pit where time should be.

Tulip

I reward myself for not thinking of him by buying tulips with breath thin petals in a bunch of eleven. I like pink, like you do, and when I stroke the closed form of each new bud, I think of you not him and I'm aware of the shift. I look at the vase of new purchases that sit on the desk as you send me a text with a tongue emoji and the words 'do you know they're edible'. The thought of a tongue inside is arousing, and you know I'm immediately parting my legs, moving my fingers, drawing an internal version of the picture you sent, petal dropping too soon.

coping strategies

I eat a banana, drink a tea which is labelled *Joy*. For a while I drank rescue remedy, six drops as opposed to four. I've stopped that now. Climax through masturbation, pink cheeks and forgetting for the time it takes. Last week I couldn't look at myself for two hours afterwards, not because I was embarrassed, but that I didn't want to see the shame.

Sex Life

After Sarah Lucas

I want to replicate this statue with you. Between your lips, the uck of suck will taste perfect, the straining of breasts under lace, the tied tip of nipples like magenta balloons about to explode, the rolling of moan that makes the lace the third person in this freeze-framed threesome. Unaware of what I'm thinking about, you are reflected in the part of bronze I look at; I imagine my mouth open with you inside, the seven images of the artist eating a banana watching from the side and for a split second of contemplation of you in my mouth, oceanic depths of unrelated and unexpected emotion are exposed. I had never thought of bronze as round until this moment, this is a juxtaposition I didn't anticipate. From this angle I am distorted, in the curve of metal flesh I am a tiny, rounded, multiplied version of self. The green of jumpsuit floral is a dull metal gun in the gaze of this bronze physical, you can't see the angled folds in waist or the catalogue way it fits the hip, or the reason I chose it

Peach

You've been away on holiday and come back with peaches wrapped in brown paper, not in a plastic box. You have selected each of the peaches individually and placed them into this sustainable packaging with hands that now stroke my inner thighs. You don't know exactly how much I've missed you and I say nothing but press your head down towards my vulva and tell you to make me come.

Page 77

She references feminism in her bio; it is, she says, her universal theme. When we see her in this scene, we don't trust her; the story she tells is implausible; she talks from an emotional perspective, she is making herself unreliable. How does the narrative show this? She lies, seems to need this. She is me. I don't trust her.

The Male Curator

After Hannah Gamble

My period impressed me, so I contacted the gallery to ask if they would display my blood on their walls. The male curator impressed me by saying yes, we'd love to see more of this, would you share further images of blood loss in toilets and clots on the Victorian tiled floor? My clotting impressed me, so I emailed him the JPEGs at 11:10pm with the subheading, 'Further Blood Imagery' and the drop of blood emoji in the subject heading. The male curator impressed me again by replying at 9:10am to say he'd just reached the office and yes, 27ml of blood loss was just what they were looking for. Would you recommend any further reading on the subject? And don't forget a 50-word bio.

Appointment

I have ticked off two thirds of the list. I compose my email to my doctor and my response reads like a prose poem which I give the title *I have all the symptoms apart from vaginal dryness*. I tell the doctor I am anxious; my periods are shortening and there is less blood each month. I use a menstrual cup, I tell the doctor proudly, so I know I am bleeding less, but no, I still have libido. I am nervous and selfish, and I don't want to look after anyone but myself and my skin is dry, but no, I am still wet inside. My response is met with silence. I wonder why sex is met with silence, and names drop from my head in the silence. I want to talk about my vagina too loudly.

Exhibit

The blood on the made-to-look Victorian floor tiles is too thick for (four ply) tissue. If I had stabbed my finger and bled this much, I'd be in Accident and Emergency by now. Instead, I am on hands and knees cleaning up the spillage of my menstrual cup. I'm at the exact gradient of the mathematics of low ache of stomach pain and bear down into a contraction style kneeling pose on the tiles which up close – too close – don't look Victorian at all.

Portrait in Mustard

1. When I walk into *Waitrose*, I collide with the burn of mustard in the bread section. It isn't the loaf I want, this sourdough with ginger which I caress to my breast, it's the feeling that I want it *more* than the sparkling water/coffee beans/tub of houmous/salt and vinegar crisps in my basket. They suddenly crowd me.

2. At first mustard doesn't appear to be overtly sexy. Not like the deep pulse purple of the knickers I bought from NET-A-PORTER for this trip to see my lover. It isn't the colour of fever that spreads in seven seconds when he licks my lips inside the satin trim of panties. When he looks at me from below, looks straight into my eyes, his lips glossed with the slip of my vulva. Is this the moment? The hottest tasting yellow on any chart.

3. There is no lipstick I want in mustard and lipstick is my usual marker of desire, just as masturbation is my *Rescue Remedy* and *Vogue*, my monthly shopping list.

4. This is the Eurostar, Paris and the Gare du Nord an hour away. In my mind I picture just how it is going to be. I'm glad I bought my *Mulberry* Lily bag in mustard and not oak. Mustard will look so much better with the four Breton tops I have brought.

5. A Schoenberg concert at Queen Elizabeth Hall. You reach for my hand as the conductor takes a bow, my tears fall *Lento*, I lick them quick into my lipstick before they drop onto your hand. This is mustard to me. This atonal bliss.

6. You feel my nipples through the mustard cashmere of my polo neck when we are in the R section of the book shop. I have *Wild Sargasso* Sea in my hand.

7. Your cock has nothing to do with mustard   or my labia   which   are cute   sugar pink   and   glisten. I've never seen mustard gleam but there is that moment you peel off my wool mustard socks   and kiss the soft part of thigh.

8. When I marry again, I'll wear a mustard velvet suit with *Louboutin* shoes, *Red Riding Hood* lips and I'll remember to wear primer this time, so I don't look shiny on the steps of City Hall.

9. The syncopation in 'America' from *West Side Story* is the purest form of mustard found to date. Nothing epitomises resilience like syncopation.

10. There is no car that looks good in this colour. This is fact. It makes me love it even more.

11. Mustard is that moment when I lift my floral dress and lean over your face.

12. If mustard could say I love you, it would feel like your hair on my hipbone on a Sunday on the first day in Spring when it rained all day.

13. Mustard is an underdog. It is plush, velvety, corduroy, never silky. It's the hint of resilience. It's the chunky cardigan with the merest flash of nipple underneath. It is the front cover of a book that you fall in love with aged twenty.

14. The bar under The Festival Hall, 9.39pm, the seat sticky from the drink I spill when you whisper in my ear and tell me what you want to do with me later in the hotel room. The hotel room has a mustard throw at the end of the bed that, even when I want you desperately, I will never put my body near.

Service Station

When you took me away to the same hotel
I had booked for my unavailable lover
I thought you looked beautiful

fragments of diamond glass upon
the light of my bifold door
how you help me as I write this

is over
this is over
this is over

you said this is like therapy but I can't think
of Warwick Services without feeling
disappointed and when I order my oat milk latte

I think of my last trip and my not yet lover's
text of apology sent when he knew
I was already on the way

the sight of my too long planned
outfit in the dirty service station glass
only made better when we go to dinner later that evening

the reservation made under his name
a cruel joke but we laughed into our Malbec and told
the waiter to keep the extra seat for our ménage à trois

I tell you I like the scent you have on and note
you are wearing the lipstick that I like best on you
cheeks perfect in Chanel Bronzing Glow

I forget the sick feeling the empty chair
has stirred up in me enjoy the erotic
pinch of suspender belt clipped marginally into flesh

I feel it again when you close the door

Cob Records

On the wall in halls is a mass-produced copy of an artwork bought from Cob Records in Lower Bangor. I fucked you under the Wednesday shadow of it for a year. Cob Records still exists, I checked online after I looked at your profile on the university's Alumni with the photo of you looking the same minus the long hair. When you went down on me that last time, I looked up at this image and wondered how a £6.99 poster knew what would happen.

You Can't Swim in a Gallery

When we go to *The Hepworth*, I go only to see *Pelagos*.
I look at it for seventeen minutes. I hear the sea.
Can you hear the sea? I ask. *It's deafening,* I say.
Too busy drowning, you do not hear.

If We Were in Llandudno

Today you ask if I remember
when we went to Llandudno for my 20th birthday.
You still have the train ticket.

Did we drink tea from polystyrene cups
or pints of snakebite? Did I wear a floral dress
like twenty-four years later

still wearing too much make up?
Your clothes fall off the same way
corduroy sounds in my mouth.

You were always writing something
political in the university newspaper office.
I wrote blank pages, drank pints, thought about how

I was falling in love with you and if
we were in Llandudno again,
I'd tell you—

Pleasure Yourself Whilst I Watch

You don't buy my favourite chocolate anymore, it is
on the list, but you say it is out of stock — that it must be
Brexit, or the fact we are over. That night, we eat
milk chocolate, and the purple of the wrapper
makes me taste copper circles of resentment when
I think about the red wrapping of our first night.
In bed, I look at your eyes fucking me, I break
into six squares, and I want to say *You forgot
my chocolate bar, you forgot my chocolate bar,*
but you are too busy in your own orgasm to notice.

Des'ree

i. I write with my rings off like I am about to play the piano. I am sat up straight in the bridge part of Des'ree's *I'm kissing you*. I am sitting up straight for the next hour thinking about

ii. in Bethnal Green I ate fast food at midnight, laid out in the middle of the bed after we drank at the bar by the tube. When we went to breakfast, I regret that I didn't sleep with ear plugs in, that I didn't tell my lover I love him. I am upset over the same thing I am always upset over. I was so proud of everything and now I am crying, and

iii. the Anaïs Nin book I read is so hot I feel like I have had four coffees. I go to bed even though it is four seventeen in the afternoon so I can

iv. think of what came first. Was it the email or the feeling when I found

v. my copy of the only Annie Ernaux I cannot read at the bottom of my Copenhagen based designer tote bag when I pack to go away. Inside is a square of card which has English Oak & Hazelnut written on one side. The square smells of nothing now, but I pretend that it smells of September and turn into a season: new duvet heavy, a fictional orange coffee. As I do this I am overcome with the taste of absence. Turn your back to me. The idea that an aged oak tree is made into a fragrance in an attempt to promise everything reminds me of a new year academic diary, whitening toothpaste, vows.

Copenhagen

Facetiming you from the pretty Scandinavian disinfected room, I tell you something which makes me wet as I say it. I am showing you how I'm using the magnified mirror to look at my vulva from the angle you would have when you go down on me. I like that my labia are the colour of the tulips on the picture in this generic hotel room. I describe what I feel, tell you to imagine mutual orgasm using no fingers, only tongue. You lick your lips. Open mouth like too ripe tulip.

[Self] Floating Form

On holiday, C and I swim topless in the sea. In the approach of a wave, I see Hepworth. In that moment of swell under the water, my breasts are sculpture proud, mounted on a personal plinth, complete, my nipples tiara against an endlessly repeated new – start sky. A plane flies overhead and I think of the times when I was cabin crew and looked down on this beach during the descent of a forty-minute flight. I wonder if looking down, I would see a [self] floating, drifting away female figure – who deliberately lets the tide remove her from the bag she leaves on the beach. Would she (I) stand up, act surprised that we (C and I) had drifted this far from where we started.

Acknowledgements and Thanks

The majority of the poems in *Portrait in Mustard* were written during my Creative Writing MA at Oxford Brookes University. With thanks to the de Rohan scholarship fund, Mary Jean Chan, Morag Joss, Jennifer Wong, Carly Schabowski, Niall Munro, and Ed Roffe.

The poems Portrait in Mustard, Apricot, Llandudno, and You Can't Swim in a Gallery placed in Cheltenham, Leeds and Wolverhampton Poetry Festival competitions.

With thanks to the editors of *Lighthouse, Poetry Ireland Review, Poetry Wales, Ambit,* and *Acropolis Journal* for publishing earlier versions of some of these poems.

To Zoë and Rhian, thank you for believing in this manuscript. I wanted this book to be about women and to be proud in its writing about sex, and between the three of us, I think we've made it that.